To _____

From _____

Because_____ is scary.
　　　　　　(scary thing)

For Lydia, Abigail, and Margaret Huck
F. P. H.

For Emma Horne
J. F.

Revised edition 2003

The Library of Congress has cataloged the first edition as follows:

Heide, Florence Parry.
Some things are scary / Florence Parry Heide ; illustrated by Jules Feiffer. — 1st ed.
p.   cm.
Summary: A list of scary things includes "skating downhill when you haven't learned
how to stop, getting hugged by someone you don't like," and "finding out your
best friend has a best friend who isn't you."
ISBN 0-7636-1222-7 (hardcover)
[1. Fear — Fiction.] I. Feiffer, Jules, ill. II. Title.
PZ7.H36 SI 2000
[E] — dc21   00-025921
ISBN 0-7636-2147-1 (revised edition)

2 4 6 8 10 9 7 5 3 1

Printed in Italy

This book was typeset in Soupbone.
The illustrations were done in watercolor with felt-tip marker.

Candlewick Press
2067 Massachusetts Avenue
Cambridge, Massachusetts 02140

visit us at www.candlewick.com

Some Things Are Scary

Florence Parry Heide

illustrated by

Jules Feiffer

Getting hugged by someone you don't like

is scary.

Stepping on
something squishy
when you're in
your bare feet

is scary.

Thinking you're not going to be picked
for either side

is scary.

Smelling a flower and finding a
bee was smelling it first

is scary.

Thinking what if you'd been
born a hippopotamus
                    is scary.

Skating downhill when you haven't learned how to stop

is scary.

Brushing your teeth with
something you thought was
toothpaste but it isn't

is scary.

Telling a lie

is scary.

Being on a swing when someone is pushing you too high

is scary.

Finding out your best friend has a best friend . . .

Playing hide-and-seek when you're it and . . .

who isn't you is scary.

you can't find anyone is scary.

Having your best friend move away

is scary.

Thinking about a big bird with big teeth
who might swoop down and carry you away

is scary.

Having to tell someone your name
and they can't understand you
and you have to spell it

is scary.

Getting scolded  is scary.

Reaching under your bed for your
shoes and grabbing something —
you don't know what —

is scary.

Being with your mother when she can't remember where she parked the car

is scary.

Thinking
you're
never
going to
get any
taller than
you are
right now

is scary.

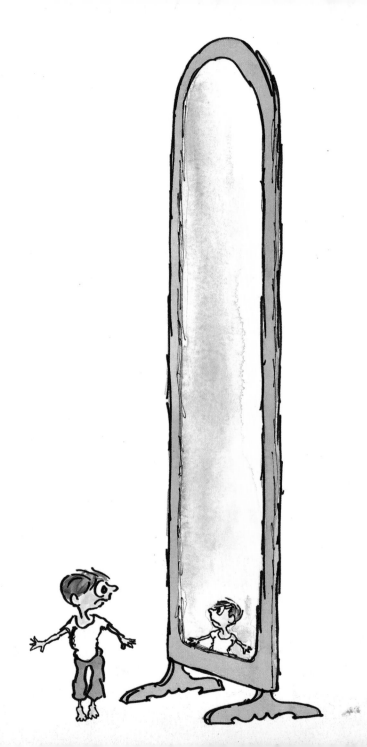

Stepping down from
something that is higher
than you thought it was

is scary.

Having people looking at you and laughing and you don't know why

is scary.

Knowing your parents are talking about you and you can't hear what they're saying

is scary.

Climbing a tree when you don't
remember how to get down

is scary.

Being with your
parents in an
art museum
and thinking
you're never
going to see
the exit sign

is scary.

Knowing
you're going
to grow up
to be a
grownup

is
scary.